Date: 3/15/12

Cat-ographies
Maine Coons
Super Big

by Nancy White

Consultant: Lynne Sherer
Judge for The International Cat Show Association (TICA)

BEARPORT
PUBLISHING

New York, New York

Credits

Cover and Title Page, © Adriano Bacchella/NaturePL/SuperStock; TOC, © Eric Isselée/Shutterstock; 4, Courtesy of The Scarborough Public Library; 5T, Courtesy of The Scarborough Public Library; 5B, © Martin Harvey/Corbis; 6, © AP Images/Reno Gazette-Journal/Andy Barron; 7, © Ulrike Schanz/Animals Animals Enterprises; 8T, © Tom Vezo/Nature Picture Library; 8B, © NaturePL/SuperStock; 9, © NaturePL/SuperStock; 10, © Richard Katris/Chanan Photography; 11L, © NaturePL/SuperStock; 11R, Courtesy of Barry Wom; 12TL, © Jeannie Harrison/Close Encounters of the Furry Kind; 12BL, © Alan Robinson/Animal-Photography; 12TR, © Alan Robinson/Animal-Photography; 12BR, © Eric Isselée/Shutterstock; 13, © Preston Smith/Preston Smith Photography; 14, © O. DIGOIT/Alamy; 15, © Tim Davis/Corbis; 16, © Juniors Bildarchiv/Age Fotostock; 17, © Toby Maudsley/Iconica/Getty Images; 18, © Jean Michel Labat/Ardea; 19, © Juniors Bildarchiv/Age Fotostock; 20, © John Daniels/Ardea; 21, © Flirt/SuperStock; 22, © Barbara O'Brien Photography; 23, Courtesy of The Scarborough Public Library.

Publisher: Kenn Goin
Editorial Director: Adam Siegel
Creative Director: Spencer Brinker
Design: Dawn Beard Creative
Photo Researcher: Omni-Photo Communications, Inc.

Library of Congress Cataloging-in-Publication Data

White, Nancy, 1942—
  Maine coons : super big / by Nancy White.
     p. cm. — (Cat-ographies)
  Includes bibliographical references and index.
  ISBN-13: 978-1-61772-142-7 (library binding)
  ISBN-10: 1-61772-142-5 (library binding)
  1. Maine coon cat—Juvenile literature. I. Title.
  SF449.M34W45 2011
  636.8'3—dc22
                    2010041167

For more information, write to Bearport Publishing Company, Inc., 101 Fifth Avenue, Suite 6R, New York, New York 10003. Printed in the United States of America in North Mankato, Minnesota.

113010
10810CGA

10 9 8 7 6 5 4 3 2 1

Contents

The Library Cat 4

Really Big! 6

Big Beginnings 8

Strong and Furry 10

Cats of Many Colors 12

Gentle Giants 14

Playful Pets 16

Longhair Care 18

Starting Out Small 20

Maine Coons at a Glance 22

Glossary 23

Index 24

Bibliography 24

Read More 24

Learn More Online 24

About the Author 24

The Library Cat

The 2010 Winterfest in Scarborough, Maine, was packed with people. During the town's winter festival, some children were ice skating while others were sledding. Near the library, kids were having an ice cube hunt. As the children played, a Maine Coon cat named Baxter walked out of the library. Everyone noticed him right away—he was almost six feet (1.8 m) tall!

Baxter with one of his friends at Winterfest

Baxter walked on two feet like a person. The cat waved to the children and blew kisses. He even did a little tap dance!

Of course, everyone knew that Baxter was not a real cat. He was a person wearing a cat costume. Baxter is the **mascot** of all the libraries in Maine.

At Winterfest, Baxter gave cans of tuna to help people who didn't have enough food to eat.

This is what a real Maine Coon cat looks like.

Baxter visits many special events all over Maine. Wherever he goes, he encourages people to get a library card, visit the library, and enjoy reading books.

Really Big!

Real Maine Coon cats cannot do the things Baxter does, and they cannot be six feet (1.8 m) tall. However, it is true that the Maine Coon cat is one of the largest **breeds** of **domestic** cats in the world.

A Maine Coon cat named Stewie holds the Guinness World Record for being the longest cat in the world. Stewie measured 48.5 inches (1.2 m) from the tip of his nose to the tip of his tail.

Maine Coons have strong muscles to support their big, heavy bodies.

While most kinds of cats weigh between 8 and 11 pounds (4 and 5 kg), Maine Coons can weigh as much as 20 pounds (9 kg). That's twice as heavy as some small dogs, such as a Chihuahua. Often standing more than 12 inches (30 cm) high at the shoulder, Maine Coons are also taller than many little dogs—as well as most other kinds of cats.

Maine Coons are naturally bigger than most cats, but if they get up to 30 pounds (14 kg), that means they are overweight. Their owners should put them on a diet.

Big Beginnings

How did Maine Coon cats get to be so big? No one knows for sure. Many cat owners think the animal's large size came about around 400 years ago. At that time, ships from Europe were coming to the **shores** of **New England**. The sailors came to trade with the **settlers** who lived there.

New England

Maine is one of the six U.S. states that make up New England.

Raccoon

Maine Coon cat

Some people think that Maine Coons are part cat and part raccoon, but that is not true. They are called "Coon cats" because their fluffy fur and big, bushy tails make them look a little like raccoons.

Cats were kept on the ships to chase rats away from the sailors' food. When the ships landed, some of the European cats wandered ashore and were left behind. Because winters in New England are so cold and harsh, only the biggest, strongest cats were able to **survive**. These large, furry cats became the **ancestors** of the Maine Coon.

Many European cats, like this Norwegian Forest cat, have long fur. The cats that came off the ships long ago may have looked like this one.

Strong and Furry

The European cats that were left behind in New England had kittens with the settlers' cats. The kittens that were small or weak couldn't live through the cold, snowy winters. However, the ones that survived were even bigger, furrier, and stronger than their European ancestors.

A Maine Coon has a long, thick, and bushy tail. The cat can wrap its tail around its body and face to keep warm.

These big cats had thick, heavy fur to keep them warm and dry. Their large, round paws with **tufts** of fur in between the toes helped them walk in deep snow. Even their ears had tufts of fur at the tips to keep the ears warm and dry. These cats were the first Maine Coons.

A Maine Coon's big paws work like snowshoes. They keep the cat's feet from sinking into the snow.

The long fur on a Maine Coon's belly protects the cat's underside from the cold, wet snow on the ground.

Cats of Many Colors

Maine Coon cats today have a long, thick, shaggy **coat**—just like the ones that lived hundreds of years ago. Yet Maine Coons don't all look alike. In fact, their fur can be almost any color that a cat can be. Maine Coons may be black, gray, or reddish-colored. Many have a **tabby**, or striped, pattern. Others are black and white, and some are even all white.

All these different-colored cats are Maine Coons.

The eyes of Maine Coon cats can also be different colors. Their big, oval-shaped eyes may be bright green, yellowish-gold, or a dark copper color. Some all-white Maine Coons have bright blue eyes. Others have one blue and one gold or green eye.

A Maine Coon whose eyes are two different colors is called "odd-eyed."

Gentle Giants

The first Maine Coon cats lived outdoors. They got food by hunting small animals such as mice. Because the cats were such good **mousers**, settlers started taking them into their homes to keep out mice. It wasn't long, however, before people found out that the cats were not only useful, they were friendly and **affectionate** as well.

Maine Coon cats don't always like sitting on people's laps, but they enjoy being petted.

Today, Maine Coon cats are popular pets. People may choose them for their size and looks, but their owners love them most for their sweet and gentle **personalities**. They get along so well with people and other pets that they are called the "gentle giants" of the cat world.

Maine Coon cats can live in a home with other pets—even dogs.

Maine Coons don't meow very much. Instead, they make a high, soft chirping sound. Many people think this small, high-pitched chirp sounds funny coming from such a large cat!

Playful Pets

Everyone likes a fun-loving pet, and Maine Coon cats love to play. That's another reason for their **popularity**. People enjoy watching big Maine Coons swatting around a little toy and pouncing on it. The cats often make their owners laugh with their scampering, tumbling, and clowning around.

Many adult Maine Coons are as playful as they were when they were kittens.

Even when they're not playing, these gentle giants like to be around people. They often follow their owners from room to room, just to be near them. Because Maine Coons enjoy being **social**, owners should remember that their pets need a lot of love, attention, and playtime.

Most cats don't like to get wet. Many Maine Coons, however, enjoy playing with water in a sink or tub. Some of them like water so much that they use their big paws to turn on a water faucet by themselves!

Longhair Care

A Maine Coon's long fur means that the pets need more **grooming** than cats that have short hair. Owners should brush and comb their Maine Coons at least once a week. Doing so not only makes the cats look good—it helps them out as well. How?

Most cats love being groomed. They let their owners know they enjoy a good brushing by purring loudly.

Like other cats, Maine Coons groom themselves by licking their fur. Unfortunately, they sometimes swallow some of it. When this happens, the long fur can get tangled into a **hairball** in the cat's stomach—and make the cat throw up. When owners brush and comb their pets, they help prevent hairballs by removing loose fur that the cats might swallow.

All cats have rough tongues that act like a hairbrush.

Maine Coons **shed** a lot of their fur in the spring when the weather starts to get warmer. For this reason, they need even more grooming during the spring and summer than at other times of the year.

Starting Out Small

When they are born, Maine Coons are no bigger than most other kinds of kittens. They are tiny enough to fit in the palm of a person's hand. Like other newborn kittens, they can't see or walk yet. About all they can do is crawl on their bellies and drink their mother's milk. However, these future giants grow fast. Six-month-old Maine Coons may weigh up to ten pounds (4.5 kg)—as much as some full-grown cats.

These kittens are about one month old. They will soon begin to run, play, and wrestle with one another.

When the kittens are 12 to 14 weeks old, they are ready to go home with their new families. The kittens' sweet and playful personalities quickly win over their owners' hearts as they grow up to be big, beautiful Maine Coon cats.

Most domestic cats are fully grown by the time they are one year old. Maine Coon cats, however, keep growing until they are three or four!

Maine Coons at a Glance

Weight:	Males weigh 15–20 pounds (7–9 kg); females weigh 9–12 pounds (4–5 kg).
Height at Shoulder:	Males are around 10–16 inches (25–41 cm) tall; females are around 8–14 inches (20–36 cm) tall.
Coat Hair:	Thick, heavy fur
Colors:	Many different colors, including white, black, brown tabby, red tabby, sliver tabby, and black and white
Country of Origin:	United States
Life Span:	Up to 15 years
Personality:	Friendly, intelligent, curious, playful; social, but not always cuddly
Special Physical Characteristics:	Large, strong body; long, heavy coat; full, fluffy tail; tufts of fur on ears and paws

Glossary

affectionate (uh-FEK-shuh-nuht) loving

ancestors (AN-sess-turz) members of a family or group who lived a long time ago

breeds (BREEDZ) particular kinds of animals

coat (KOHT) the fur on a cat or other animal

domestic (duh-MESS-tik) animals bred and tamed for use by humans; not wild

grooming (GROOM-ing) brushing and cleaning an animal

hairball (HAIR-bawl) a clump of fur that gets stuck in a cat's stomach

mascot (MASS-kot) an animal that represents an organization, a team, or other group

mousers (MOUSS-urz) cats that are good at catching and killing mice

New England (NOO ING-gluhnd) a region of the Northeastern United States made up of six states: Maine, New Hampshire, Vermont, Massachusetts, Rhode Island, and Connecticut

personalities (*pur*-suh-NAL-uh-teez) the combinations of qualities or traits that make one person or animal different from others

popularity (*pop*-yuh-LAIR-uh-tee) being liked by many people

settlers (SET-luhrz) people who go to live and make their homes in a new place

shed (SHED) to have fur or hair fall off the body

shores (SHORZ) land along the edges of lakes, rivers, or oceans

social (SOH-shuhl) friendly; happy and comfortable when spending time with people

survive (sur-VIVE) to stay alive in a difficult situation or environment

tabby (TAB-ee) having fur with a striped pattern

tufts (TUFTS) small clumps

Index

Baxter 4–5, 6
coat 12, 22
colors 12–13, 22
ears 11, 22
eyes 13
fur 8–9, 10–11, 12, 18–19, 22
grooming 18–19

hairballs 19
height 7, 22
hunting 14
kittens 10, 16, 20–21
life span 22
New England 8–9, 10

Norwegian Forest cat 9
paws 11, 17, 22
personality 14–15, 16–17, 21, 22
playfulness 16–17, 20–21, 22
raccoons 8

settlers 8, 10, 14
shedding 19
size 6–7, 8, 10, 15, 20–21, 22
tails 6, 8, 10, 22
water 17
weight 7, 20, 22
Winterfest 4–5

Bibliography

Daly, Carol Himsel, DVM, and Karen Leigh Davis. *Maine Coon Cats: A Complete Pet Owner's Manual.* Hauppauge, NY: Barron's Educational Series (2006).

Hornidge, Marilis. *That Yankee Cat: The Maine Coon.* Gardiner, ME: Tilbury House (2002).

Read More

Mattern, Joanne. *The Maine Coon Cat.* Mankato, MN: Capstone Press (2001).

Quasha, Jennifer. *Maine Coon Cats.* New York: Rosen (2000).

Scheunemann, Pam. *Marvelous Maine Coons.* Edina, MN: ABDO (2010).

Learn More Online

To learn more about Maine Coon cats, visit
www.bearportpublishing.com/Cat-ographies

About the Author

Nancy White has written many children's books about animals. She lives in New York's Hudson River Valley. Her cat, Buddy, sits on her desk and keeps her company while she is writing.